How to Live your Life Dreams in Abundance and Prosperity.

Introduction

Dear Reader,

Everything in your life is a result of what you know, what you experience and how you interact with your consciousness. These elements make up the ultimate source from which everything else evolves.

Learning about yourself can be the most fascinating endeavor one can imagine. Manifesting is an ability of consciousness at the inner level, and is not determined by any outer circumstances. We all share the same inner source; no one gets more or less. The only difference is that some people are more aware of it than others. However, with this report and with a positive attitude to learn, you can go as deeply down into the rabbit hole as you wish. The rabbit hole is an analogy for your willingness to explore the unknown.

The more you know about the unknown the more you actually understand how little you know. It makes you humble and brings you back to the world of wonders, miracles and magic.

A world in which everything is possible.

The Power of Experiencing your own Knowledge

Life is all about experience. All your knowledge is worthless if you don't *apply* it in your life. Experience is created by applying what you know. It's the difference between knowing how an apple tastes and eating an apple. If you have never tasted an apple and someone tells you how it tastes, you will only have a limited knowledge of it. However when you actually taste an apple, you experience it for yourself. Nobody can take this experience away from you. Just imagine if you only had the knowledge of how an apple tastes and a few people came by to tell you that it really tastes differently. What would you do? You would have your own experience no longer being confused by others. This is the power of your own experience.

If you understand and follow the basics of what is outlined here, you will become the master of your life by manifesting it, exactly as you wish. Within yourself, you will create the ability to deal with any challenges you may face and find the answer to lasting happiness.

Enjoy reading . . .

Table of Contents

Introduction 3

Exploring the Source of Happiness 7

The Importance of Knowing What You Want From Life 11

Find Your Unique Strengths, Gifts And Talents 15

Finding The Courage to Step Out of Normality 19

Attention – The Infinite Source of Your Potential 21

Imagination - Your Magic Virtual Reality World 26

Your Beliefs - Concepts That Create Your Experience 30

10 Impeding Beliefs that Prevent You From Getting Rich 34

Quantum Physics - The New 21st Century Life Paradigm 37

What is The Law of Attraction? 42

A Spiritual Viewpoint of Free Will 44

The Ultimate Question - Free Will Versus Destiny? 46

Intention – Aim For Your Goals 50

Creating Your Intentions – Worksheet 57

Why Your Attitude Makes A Difference 59

Conclusion – The Art of Manifesting 60

The Ultimate Life Fulfillment - Serving Others 64

Exploring the Source of Happiness

Every single person on this planet is striving to be happy. This is the state of being that we all know from the time of our birth. It is a state of being that we recognize as our true self – who we deeply are.

Now, for most of us, this happiness doesn't last. It gets replaced by a striving force to survive, which feels more like the opposite of being happy. The reason we are doing this is astonishingly simple – *because we are told to do so.*

- Our heritage tells us what to think and feel
- Our government tells us what to think and feel
- Our society tells us what to think and feel

Our current world view is determined by a centuries old paradigm – Newton's world view of the universe as a giant clock works is studied, as it has been for centuries, in our schools. This world-view teaches us that we humans operate similarly to a mechanical clock. This view teaches that everything is ruled by cause and effect, and almost everything can be replaced when it's damaged. In addition, we are taught the concept of the survival of the fittest. Together, these two ideas condition us to accept that people, like animals, must function in a state of mechanical perfection or be replaced by more perfectly functioning components in the system.

These old concepts have led to a society that is completely self-centered, ego-driven, irresponsible and environmentally destructive. They have led us to a cult of happiness seekers who get their adrenalin rush by buying more useless stuff on a daily basis – all in a subconscious attempt to maintain the illusion of perfection.

We have been conditioned to consume the world in an effort to attain this illusory perfection, and it shows in our day-to-day lives. Simply put, we work at places we don't like in order to buy stuff we don't need.

We have forgotten that the source of happiness lies within the center of our spiritual being, and we have replaced it by seeking it in the material world. We have things backward.

What is the Manifesting Process?

Where does it initially come from: Desire? Wanting something? Bettering ourselves?

Take a good look at your life right now. Where do you live? What does your furniture look like? What kind of car do you drive? How much money is in your bank account? Look in the mirror – how do you look? Everything has been manifested one way or the other, by you. You may not be aware of how far-reaching your ability to manifest truly is in all its aspects.

Have My Thoughts Created All This?

Yes! Whatever you see in the physical universe has been created in one way or the other by your thoughts. Your thoughts are the blueprints of what later becomes physical form. Everything starts with an idea, which is a thought. That's why it is crucial to pay attention to your thoughts.

If you worry about getting all those bills paid you will create more of the same thing, simply because you have thought about it. Your thoughts are nothing more than frequencies or vibrations that resonate with similar vibrations already existing. Place two guitars side by side and pluck a string on one. The string on the other guitar will start vibrating, even though you haven't touched it. It is the principle of resonance. Fascinating, isn't it?

You *want* to be able to control your thoughts, given that they create your reality. If you can control your thoughts, you can control what you want to create and manifest in your life. If you can't control your thoughts, things will manifest that seem random and unconnected to you – and they are – they are actually manifested from other people.

Your consciousness is like a radio station. You can send signals and programs and you can receive signals and programs. Sometimes you may want to receive and sometimes you may want to send. To know when to send and when to receive is one of the greatest success factors in life. It is the balance of knowing when to create and when to experience. You cannot constantly create for you would miss out on the other part of the experience. On the other hand, if you only experience things, you will never get to manifest anything.

Another way of putting it would be *responsive responsibility* – the ability to *consciously respond*. In every moment, you have a choice about what you want to do, and what you want to decide. If you don't exercise this power nothing happens in your life – at least not what you want. This brings us to the next topic.

The Importance of Knowing What You Want From Life

Most people never think about what they want in their lives. They live without this knowledge or forethought and become victims of their own circumstance. Work is just about a job – to get by financially. Life becomes a series of issues like choosing to live somewhere because the rent is cheap, never understanding how to be in relationships or becoming ineffectual parents. The list goes on and on. Within yourself there is a craving for more. Is it substance, contact or a deeper understanding of life? No one has ever introduced such people to the concept of endless possibility. "As a man thinketh, so is he."

A major key to manifesting the life you want is to ponder what you want out of life. What is it that you want to do with your life? A good exercise is to take a piece of paper and write down the answers to the following questions:

- What is my deepest desire?
- What would I like to accomplish in my life?
- What would I like to accomplish this year?
- Where would I like to be in 5 years?
- Where would I like to be in 20 years?
- What am I good at?

Look into all areas of your life:

- Your profession
- Your relationships
- Your health
- Your financial situation
- How you have fun (how you spend your holidays)

Do you Spend Enough Time with your Goals – Are they Important?

After you have written down a list of what you would like to accomplish in your life, you will want to set priorities for them. Just take the list that you wrote down and give each topic 1-5 points. 1 being the least important to 5 points being the most. Now you have priorities in your life, which will help you decide where you want your attention to be.

It is a simple equation: understand simply that you want to spend most of your time with the number one topic on your list. Spend slightly less time with the number two entry on your list – and so on for numbers three through five. There is no need to slice up the day in time slots. Simply by doing this exercise you are programming your consciousness to spend time according to your list.

Let's assume you would like to find your life partner in the next two years, and that this is your primary goal, at the very top of your list. When you check your thought process at the end of the day and you find that you have not spent most of your free time addressing this goal, you have a misalignment, and you may never reach your goal. When this happens simply recognize it and adjust accordingly.

Working all day only to sit on your couch and watch TV will not get you where you want to be. You must take action to manifest your goal(s), for example:

- Take action by signing up for a dance class
- Book a weekend seminar on a subject that intrigues you
- Attend a workshop that focuses on your interest
- Spend time at places where you can meet people

If your goal happens to be that you want to be a millionaire within five years, and you are spending only five minutes of your time each day to accomplish this goal, then don't be surprised if your financial situation never changes.

There is another important aspect of manifestation here that requires consistency. Let's assume you have made your priority list and everything on your list feels good so far. It is very important that you are in emotional agreement with your goals – they must feel right to you. If you simply create goals in your mind that are not of value to you then you will find yourself having a hard time working to achieve them.

What happens with most people's scenario is that they have a goal that feels right for them, then they start working on their goal. In other words, they put their attention into making their goal a reality. A few weeks pass by and nothing happens. Now discouragement sets in and the goal somehow seems unreachable, the motivation is down to zero.

This is the point where you must *feel* your discouragement. Don't just put it away or ignore it – face it as completely and consciously as you can. This might be unpleasant for you but it will help you get closer to your goal. How is this? When you want to change your reality you obviously need to do something differently than what you have done before. So this is where the reality check comes in. You look around and cannot see any change. But changes may have already occurred in your thinking and behavior. You may have set things in motion that you cannot yet see.

Discouragement sets in when you assume that things should be happening sooner than you are ready for them. Remember – there are no unrealistic goals, only unrealistic time frames. So feel your discouragement and let it dissolve. Look at what you have done and realign your strategies. If one way does not lead to success don't give up at that point – simply try another. If you stick to a goal you will reach it.

Sometimes you may push too hard when you just need to let go and take the pressure off. You doubt yourself at this point, believing there is nothing you can accomplish. Go to the place in your mind where you *know* you can't fail. Reading a book or watching a motivational movie may help to get you realigned with your powerful source.

Find Your Unique Strengths, Gifts And Talents

Most successful people have something in common. They love what they do. You won't find rich and successful people that hate what they do.

Each of us is unique, having specific talents and gifts. It is something innately inherent in all of us, a combination of energy patterns leading towards a natural affinity for certain subjects in life, certain ways of being. One of the most important tasks in your life is to find these talents and gifts within yourself, which is a recognition of what you have brought into your creation.

Let's assume that you are given a hammer without having any knowledge of how to utilize this tool. Stay with me now – this is a gross over-simplification of an extremely important aspect of your reality. You are given nails but you use the wrong end of the hammer. You can't see any success with accomplishing your task of hammering in the nails. You have the tool but not the knowledge of its correct application. Similarly, how can we manage our lives without understanding the many tools available and their practical applications? You might even have a moment of enlightened clarity. We can all relate to finally understanding something that had been tripping us up. Wouldn't it be nice if someone had shared the necessary information beforehand – before experiencing frustration and possibly giving up?

Recognizing your own strengths and talents is absolutely essential for any further steps you take in life. Writing them down should make them more real to you if you're not used to thinking about them. If you know your distinctive strengths and talents you should be able to write them down in a few sentences without having to think too much about the process.

If you are not sure, or you really have no clue, here are a few tips that will help you identify them:

Think back to your childhood:
- What were the toys you liked to play with?
- What were you interested in?
- What did you like best to play?
- What presents did you wish to receive for your birthday and Christmas?
- What did you dream of becoming in your future?

Ask your Closest Friends

Tell your friends that you want to re-evaluate your talents and you need an honest opinion from them. Make sure to ask your friends to be 100% honest with you. Allow them to take a fresh look at you and ask them to forget all about what you are doing professionally – keep it on a personal level.

- What do your friends think you are good at?
- What do they think your talents are?
- What do they recommend what you should do with your life?

Ask Yourself a Few Questions

Take a notebook and read through these questions. Make sure you open up your mind and allow these questions to solidify in your imagination. Don't take these questions too seriously, play with them and also write down what comes up spontaneously – these are sometimes the most profound answers.

These questions are designed to expand your consciousness out of the normal mindset. The best solutions are always found outside the normal realm of thinking. Remember, your mind is part of the collective consciousness; therefore you have access to all information. Your mind is connected to the infinite source of all existence.

- What would you do if you had enough money not to work ever again?
- What were your dreams when you were younger?
- What do you think is impossible for you to do?
- What would you do if you won five million dollars?
- What would you do if this was the last day of your life?
- What would you do if you couldn't fail?
- What are your strengths and talents?
- Do you have a wish but don't know how to fulfill it?
- What do you admire most about others?
- What would your ideal lifestyle look like?
- What does success mean for you?
- What makes you really happy?
- Is there anything that needs to be invented?
- What does a perfect day look like for you?
- What would you do if there were no restrictions?
- What really excites you?
- What would you be honored and recognized for?
- Where do you see your life in ten years?
- If you were immortal, what would you do with your life?
- What needs to change to make this a better world?
- What would you do if you were Superman?
- What are you proud of?
- What would you do if you were the President?
- What would you like to accomplish this year?
- What would you do differently if you could start over again?

Finding your strengths and talents is like first building the basement for your house. It is your foundation. It is like the soil from which a strong and beautiful tree can grow. It provides you with your unique potential. It is the unique gift that came with you when you were born. You are being asked here to nourish it until it is strong enough to guide you in your life.

Don't waste your time chasing someone else's dream or goal or anything that is not given to you that you cannot claim first as your own. Use the talents you came in with or the ones you developed along the way. You may become very good at something but you will never find true, lasting happiness with it if you can't own it completely. You will always have to compensate with something else so as not to feel the void in your life – a void that is only filled by your own inherent strengths and talents. If you don't know your talents and strengths, make getting to know them your major task in life.

Use whatever tools you feel comfortable with. Try to find a way to dig deeper into yourself. This is your life – and you're worth it! If you feel comfortable with astrology schedule a private session with a professional astrologer. You will be amazed how much you can find out about yourself in just an hour.

Finding The Courage to Step Out of Normality

If you have found your talents and strengths, you know you are unique. It gives you confidence and a sense of stability. That doesn't mean that you go around telling people how different you are. It is just a recognition of what you brought into this lifetime.

Make a commitment to follow these gifts and talents; let them guide you. Don't let anybody tell you what you should do. Don't let anybody tell you that you are not good enough to fulfill your dreams. Identify as much as possible with your dreams, as they are the surest guides in your life. They will show you where to go.

There is no guarantee at all that everything will be fine and easy when you follow your dreams. It may be the opposite. You may find yourself alone in the world with the feeling that everyone else is doing the right thing but you.

Your gifts, talents and strengths are your ultimate potential, but they can also be your pitfalls. You will need to cultivate them over time. In the beginning they are also your weaknesses and you will be tested by them. The more you withstand them, the stronger they grow inside you, until they become your life force.

Contemplate: What if you have chosen your gifts in your last life?

A little story about this: A soul is ready to incarnate to earth and gets sent to the 'feelings' supermarket where it can chose what dominant feeling it wants to carry into its incarnation. The soul enters the store and finds that all feelings except one are sold out for today! Only one is left and it is labeled *Betrayal*. As a soul, all feelings are equal and there are no judgments or preferences. The soul takes *Betrayal* and enters its life on earth to experience this feeling in all its variations.

What's the point, you may ask? Knowing your purpose, even if it involves so-called negative experience at a fundamental level, will free you from becoming a victim. You will have the understanding that you chose this. Therefore, you can grow with the experience and ultimately get the teaching you need to learn, the understanding and wisdom you desired to attain. There are no mistakes, only opportunities. Every single person has a different path on earth. If you understand your path it doesn't matter what it is, and you will not be jealous that others have more – which, after all, are only just different paths. You will have a profound understanding that what you do is exactly the right thing – no matter what it is.

It doesn't matter if you have a small or a big house. It does not matter if you have more or less money than others. Being on your unique path is where you belong; it is the only way to get to your unique dreams.

Attention – The Infinite Source of Your Potential

Attention is probably the most important gift you possess. The word *attention* comes from the Latin *attendere*, which means, "to turn one's mind towards" – to turn one's mind or perhaps one's senses; the act or state of applying the mind to an object of sense or thought.

It is the act of taking possession by the mind, in clear and vivid form, of one of several simultaneously possible objects or trains of thought. It implies withdrawal from some things in order to deal effectively with others.

Our faculty of attention affects us in countless ways. Our very perception of reality is tied closely to where we focus our attention. Only what we pay attention to seems real to us, whereas whatever we ignore – no matter how important it may be – seems to fade into insignificance.

Each of us chooses, by our way of *attending* to things, the universe we inhabit and the people we encounter. But for most of us, this "choice" is unconscious, so it's not really a choice at all. When we think about who we are, we can't possibly remember all the things we've experienced, all the behaviors and qualities we have exhibited. What comes to mind when we ask "Who am I?" Those things consist of what we have been paying attention to over the years. The same goes for our impressions of other people. The reality that appears to us is not so much what's out there, as it is those aspects of the world we have focused on.

What we *look at* may not be what we *attend to*. It is possible to look in one direction but actually notice changes in another direction. Overt attention is the act of directing our eyes or ears towards a stimulus source. Covert attention is the act of mentally focusing on a particular stimulus. Basically, you can direct your attention towards the outside world or towards the world within. You can observe – *attend to* – your thoughts!

Mastering and controlling your attention gives you the freedom to choose what happens in your life. There are countless things happening at the same time all over the world, however, as long as your attention is not directed to any of it – nothing really happens for you.

> **Contemplate:** When you close your eyes is the world still there? What evidence do you have to prove it on your own?

This is very important to understand. The more you can control your attention the more you attract only the things in your life that you really want. If you do not pay attention to the crime scene on your television it does not create this reality for you. If you don't pay attention to negative things in your life it will not create that reality. This doesn't mean you should ignore the parts of the world that do not produce peace and happiness for you; it simply means not to give them too much attention. Don't get absorbed in them – decide when enough is enough and move on to something you want your attention to be focused on, for example, the important goals and dreams of your life.

Life is not what you see on TV nor what you hear and read in the news!

An analogy for attention is the faucet in your garden. You open it and see an endless stream of water flowing. Now you connect to it a hose, and with this hose you are able to direct the flow of water anywhere you decide. You may decide to water your rosebush in the back. You take the hose and direct it toward the rosebush and water it. Now, what happens when your hose has holes and leaks? Let's assume for this analogy that your hose is really old and that there are many holes and leaks. The water is our analogy for the free attention you have in life. Taking a close look at the hose reveals that it is leaking in several places, and that the water is missing your rosebush entirely but plenty is flowing down into the earth to nourish the weeds that are dormant and only need a good drink to begin to sprout. If you look at the end of the hose you will notice there is not much water left for the rosebush.

Two things are happening here:

1. Your attention goes somewhere you would rather not have it go and things are happening that you *don't want* to have happen.
2. Your attention is not focused enough to have an effect on what you *do want* to accomplish.

Do you see how important it is to train your attention? There are many exercises you can do. One simple method is to simply observe your attention and to speak out loud where it is in the moment. You may do this when you are alone until you get comfortable with yourself. This is a funny exercise and you may find yourself laughing.

Here is what it might look like:
- I am thinking about tomorrow . . .
- There is a cat next to me . . .
- What I am doing here . . . ?
- So many thoughts . . .
- Am I crazy . . . ?
- The carpet is brown . . .
- It's dirty too . . .
- I should get it cleaned . . .
- Ah, just relax . . .
- How busy my mind is . . .
- What's next . . .

You may find yourself thinking about how crazy this is, but this exercise actually just happens in a short time span of your attention. You may have a few thousand of these each day . . . no wonder some people feel constantly stressed, overwhelmed and light years away from their goals (*if they have any*)!

Do this every day for about 15 minutes and you will observe that several things happen. First of all, your mind gets calmer but at the same time may also feel exhausted, especially after the first few times you do the exercise. Exhausting your attention is a very interesting occurrence that happens quite often and naturally in your daily life. Training your mind not to exhaust itself will sharpen your focus and free up your attention considerably.

The more free attention you have, the happier you feel and the more power you have to control what is happening in your life.

In Summary

You have infinite attention; however you can exhaust your attention to the degree that there isn't anything left. Be aware of how you use your attention. Learn to deliberately choose where you want to place your attention.

What Absorbs Your Attention?

We need to pay attention to things in our daily lives; everything we do requires that of us. Businesses vie for our attention. The ubiquitous backdrop of advertising that surrounds us is constantly trying to get our attention. The more aware we are of it the more we can deliberately decide not to give our attention away.

The following is a list of the most powerful attention suckers:

- Television, especially advertising and news channels
- Newspapers
- Billboards
- Shopping malls
- People telling you stories you are not interested in
- Arguments
- Large crowds
- Excessive and loud noises
- Self-criticism
- Driving on the freeway
- Email spam
- Junk mail

Contemplate: Where does (your) attention come from?

Imagination

Your Magic Virtual Reality World

The act of imagining is another wonderful ability of your consciousness. Even with open eyes you can imagine springtime in the fields, the fresh scents, the birds chirping, the warmth of the sun. You can even imagine that you are sitting in the grass and feel the wind blowing through your hair. You can imagine touching the soul, letting it rinse through your hands.

You are able to imagine objects that do not exist, and you can imagine that these objects do whatever you decide. They don't have to follow any physical rules. Many inventors have used the power of imagination to think up ideas for new products, machines and improvements.

The most interesting part is that these imaginings, once you have made them, become part of your memory! It's like a virtual world that does not follow any rules that currently exist – it is the ultimate playing field in cyber space.

Imagination is also very powerful in memorizing things that you normally could not remember. Here is a simple example. For now, just read it:

There is a red ball. On the left side of the red ball is a green ball and on the right side of the red ball is a blue ball. Next to the blue ball is a yellow ball and next to the green ball is a white ball. On the left side of the white ball is a black ball and on the right side of the yellow ball is an orange ball.

Now repeat what you just read without looking at it . . .

Without the use of your imagination you probably won't be able to memorize this. Now do it again, but this time you will use the power of your imagination. Just imagine that you are at a billiard table. Read the instructions again, but this time visualize each ball lying on the pool table.

There is a red ball. On the left side of the red ball is a green ball and on the right side of the red ball is a blue ball. Next to the blue ball is a yellow ball and next to the green ball is a white ball. On the left side of the white ball is a black ball and on the right side of the yellow ball is an orange ball.

Okay, now close your eyes and recall the picture of the billiard balls on the pool table. Without reading the instructions again you will probably remember every ball position.

By using your imagination you have expanded your brain capacity in terms of how your brain stores information. You have used the left and the right hemisphere of your brain together. One hemisphere is the more logical side the other half is the more artistic side. When both hemispheres work together the brain is able to store the information in its long-term memory. From there it is accessible at any time, even after many years have passed. If you only use one side of your brain the information takes a longer time to get to your long-term memory – usually only effectively by repeating the task. Most of the time the information gets stored only in short-term memory and is no longer available after a day or so.

There are basically only three methods to store information in your long-term memory:

1. Repetition
2. Intensity
3. Using both sides of the brain simultaneously

What Does Imagination have To Do With Manifesting?

If you can imagine it, it will not be difficult to create it. Let's assume you want $20,000 in your bank account by the end of this month. Start using your imagination:

- Visualize your bank statement reading your balance is $20,000
- Visualize making a withdrawal and you are holding $20,000 in your hand
- Visualize how you feel
- Visualize bringing the money home and spreading it all over your table
- Visualize what you can buy with this money

By doing this process you are already training your mind for the event of claiming $20,000. Your mind will start bringing up other pictures and stories when you do this exercise.
For example the following can happen:

- A thought comes up – *Ah, how bogus this is!*
- A thought comes up – *I don't believe this will ever happen!*
- A thought comes up – *Why not go for $50,000 or $100,000?*
- A feeling arises – you feel excited
- A feeling arises – you feel unmotivated
- A pictures arises – you only see $850 in your bank account
- A picture arises – you cannot see a number on your bank statement

These are all uncertainties of the mind that will vanish when you do the exercise several times. Do it often, until you see exactly what you desire as actually happening. Do it until there is no other thought, feeling or picture coming up that is not aligned with your goal.

How to Fire Walk over Chalk

I once participated in a fire walk ritual as part of a weekend self exploration course. The goal for the evening was to walk over a 30-foot long, 190-degree, hot pathway of chalk. I had only to put my hand over the chalk to immediately know "absolutely" that walking on this infernal path would be impossible without instantly and painfully burning my feet.

To prepare for this experience we were told to visualize the walk over the fire and use our imagination to eliminate any obstacles our minds could come up with. Somehow, I ended up visualizing a lava field that I was walking through. It took me four of five virtual walk-throughs until my mind no longer clung to the idea that my feet were burning.

It took me another two or three mental walk-throughs until I felt totally comfortable. In the last visualization I even ended up waking over the fire twice as I could not believe it the first time or two. Guess what happened on that evening? After watching about seven or eight other people do the walk, it was my turn. I positioned myself at the beginning, calmed my mind and started to walk slowly in little steps over the fire. At the end I couldn't believe what I just did and I walked all the way back over it again!

No burns, nothing! However, I could feel the energy of the fire on my feet. Needless to say, not all the people finished their walks successfully. Some were very badly burned indeed. I will never forget this experience as it helped me tremendously in understanding the power of visualization.

Your Beliefs

Concepts That Create Your Experience

Beliefs are basically concepts that we either make up on our own or that we take over from someone else. The function of believing something is another great ability of your consciousness. The idea of belief that we talk about here has nothing to do with the kind of belief that is usually used in a religious context.

Belief is a built-in function of your consciousness. It is one of the most powerful instruments to shape your reality. It is so powerful that, when adaptively formulated from many people, it can shift mass consciousness and lead to profound changes in our society. It even has the power to shift the collective consciousness of the whole of civilization on this planet.

What is the Purpose of a Belief?

The purpose of a belief is to make an experience. How is this possible? A belief is basically a concept, something that you assume, but actually don't know as a concrete fact. You only know something for sure when you have experienced it. Everything else are concepts that we consider to comprise the basis of our knowledge. Our whole life is built around beliefs.

There are two different ways you can live your life. The first way is to observe nature and then construct a belief around it. This is still currently the way we receive information in school; it is what operates most prevalently in people's lives. The problem with this approach is that it leads to a form of living that convinces us that we are not responsible for anything that happens in our lives. This approach also leads to the idea that we cannot change things in our lives.

The second way is the opposite – you decide what you want to believe and later find the evidence of this belief in nature. Does this sound strange to you? Maybe not, maybe you already have shifted your consciousness into this new way of thinking.

What are the Benefits of Thinking this Way?

You are responsible for what is happening in your life. You could also say that you have created it one way or another. Either you are conscious of being your life's creator or you are not. A lot of what we actually create happens unconsciously. Another benefit of thinking this way – i.e., consciously – is that you can change what you like to experience by simply changing your beliefs and the concepts around them. Understand how powerful this is! When you live your life as the master of your beliefs you can handle anything because you ultimately know that you have created it. And even if you are not aware, you will at some point accept it.

By the act of believing we form a unique structure in our consciousness, an energy pattern that acts like a blueprint for what we will experience in our life.

Let's look at a practical example to illustrate this point. Just imagine you are at home and your doorbell rings. You open the door and there is a man you have never seen before. He starts telling you his story about having lost his home and his job and how he needs money to survive. He asks you if you can spare a few dollars.

During the conversation your consciousness is automatically processing the information. There are probably thousands of things happening in your mind in a fraction of a second. Your mind looks into its memory banks to find similar experiences. A similar experience makes it easy to act on the current situation in the same way. Your mind will also find all kinds of stories that have to do with money. Your mind observes the man and tries to categorize the whole situation.

- Is this man trustworthy?
- Is this man telling the truth?
- Do I want to give him money?
- How much money do I want to give?

Finally you have to make up your mind. You have a choice of what to do – *you always have a choice*. You can simply react to the situation and let your mind tell you what to do, by calling on one of the thoughts that automatically came up to guide you. Or you can deliberately make a choice by either believing his story or not. At this point you have no evidence if his story is true or not. You may not even be interested in his story, or the decision to give him the money.

Reaction Versus Action

A reaction is an unconscious response to a given situation. Your consciousness is not involved and the outcome is random. Most of the time it is an answer that reflects what you have done in the past. It is a choice-less and powerless approach to handling a situation.

An action is a deliberate choice you make. It is a response to a situation that is based on the result of consciously analyzing and contemplating a given situation. It empowers you and moves your life further along the path you have chosen.

Your action and the outcome of this situation are completely separate from and different from the idea of whether you believe him or not. Beliefs are very powerful. One way to determine what beliefs you want to take on is simply by looking for what the reality would be, that this belief would create. Is this belief supporting what I would like to experience or not?

Many of our beliefs are carried forward from our parents, from school, from friends and from news sources like radio and television. You have a choice to make about taking these beliefs on unfiltered, or by evaluating them and either accepting or rejecting them.

You will also experience that it is more important to understand *how you believe*, than *what your belief is*. Understanding the process of how you believe gives you tremendous power in your life. You will find that different sources of news are more or less credible to your beliefs. If your best friend tells you something you may believe it instantly, as you have known your friend for years and, in the past, your friend's information was always reliable. Getting information from strangers is a totally different story and the level of acceptance may be much lower. Take doctors, for example. Most people willingly adopt the beliefs of their doctors quite thoroughly as they may see their physicians as the ultimate truth givers.

If you hold a belief that you "know" to be true, you have assigned that belief the highest level of trustworthiness. However, understand that it is still a belief and not the truth. The truth-as-absolute does not exist, even if you find all the evidence in the world for it. You will discover this in one of the next chapters when we talk about quantum physics.

10 Impeding Beliefs
that Prevent You From Getting Rich

At one point in your life, you may ask yourself why other people are so successful with money when you are not. Depending on how closely you look, you will have several answers. Do these sound familiar?

- They're just luckier than I am
- They have a better education than I do
- They were born into a rich family
- They are white and have better opportunities than I do
- They already had the money to start a business
- They already had the money to invest in real estate
- They are smarter than I am
- They are younger than I am
- They look better than I do
- They probably work harder than I do

The list probably continues to fill several pages. Money is the topic that generates the most beliefs, followed by the topic of relationship. I once led a seminar where we investigated people's beliefs about money. After only 30 minutes we came up with three full pages!

You may not know this yet, but your beliefs are the blueprint for your reality. If you knew that, would you deliberately create one from the list above? Probably not, because these beliefs are not supportive at all. These beliefs create a reality that leaves you 'playing' the victim, and furthermore, keeps you right where you are. You are not improving your life one bit.

Why are we creating these beliefs in the first place, when we know that they are not constructive at all? The answer lies in the nature of our consciousness. Most of us were told that there is a universe out there and this universe shapes our reality. It is the basic belief that life happens to us. Most of us get these beliefs confirmed several times per day. The result is that our consciousness gets imprinted each day with the same message. The message with the same old belief.

Meanwhile, as adults, we are not even aware that our life, 'as it happens' is built around a belief. It becomes a profound reality that we prove to ourselves in each moment.

So how do we get out of this dilemma? We need to take a step back and look at our beliefs. Take a piece of paper and a pencil and write down all the beliefs you have around money. Don't think too much, be spontaneous. When you have run out of your own beliefs, think about what other people's beliefs are about money.

Then mark each belief with an 'I' or an 'S' depending if the belief is *impeding* or *supportive*. Impeding beliefs do not support creating wealth, supportive beliefs do. Now, look at your list and count each supportive and impeding belief. What is your score? How many impeding beliefs do you have, and how many supportive beliefs do you have?

Realize that all the impeding beliefs do not support the creation of fortune. Now, take a new piece of paper, and brainstorm beliefs that will exactly create the wealth you would like to have. When you are done with the list, go over each of your new beliefs and create a mental image. Hold this mental image for at least 10-20 seconds. You may need some practice, but every time you do it, you will get better at it. Do this exercise in a quiet, calm and relaxed environment, as this will help to imprint these beliefs into your consciousness.

Remember, beliefs are the blueprint of what will manifest in your life. With a little training, you will be able to move onto the next stage, which is feeling your beliefs. Feel as if these new beliefs, that foster what you really want to create, have actually been manifested.

- How does it feel to be a millionaire?
- How does it feel to have abundance in your life?
- How does it feel to have more money than you can spend?
- How does it feel to give to others?
- How does it feel to buy something without having to look at the price?

Whenever you catch yourself thinking or speaking an impeding belief about money, stop what you are doing. Go back to the place in your mind where you recall one of your deliberately created beliefs about money, and connect with it. The more you do this, the more you will train your mind to think in a new way, a way that leads to living an abundant and prosperous life.

Quantum Physics -
The New 21st Century Life Paradigm

We are in the midst of one of the most significant paradigm shifts mankind has ever encountered. We are seeing the end of Newton's mechanical world-view, which is being replaced by a new one that tells us we are nothing more then interconnected consciousness, and that matter is nothing more than a form of energy.

The Age of Newton's Mechanical Clockwork

For more than two hundred years Newton's ideas dictated our world view. Newton declared that everything operates mechanically and can be predicted like clockwork. Science in Newton's view, being nothing more than the act of observing, meant that this world view was easily perpetuated by independent observers all over the world.

In the late 19th century, science entered into the era of subatomic physics, which changed everything. Scientists discovered that the so-called 'subatomic particles' were not particles at all. They behaved like particles when they were measured but they traveled like waves.

Quantum theory has changed everything, because what was once a mechanical, external universe has now become a web of intelligence. *Science finally admits that the simple act of observing changes the result of any experiment, and by extension, that the observer and the observed are not separate.*

What follows from this new understanding is a completely different way of dealing with the world we perceive. Our old model of an objective world view has to be replaced with a new model that states everything is subjective, the observer influencing the observed.

The Quantum Paradox – The Wave-Particle Duality

Wave-Particle Duality is perhaps the most notable concept of the quantum world; and by extension, it is also the philosophical basis of modern thought. It is the defining characteristic of elementary physical entities, such as electrons, protons, neutrons, atoms, and molecules, which exist on the one hand in states which behave like waves when they are not observed, and on the other hand behave like particles when observed.

The key is in the observation. In its wave-like state, the physical structure is typically extended in space, but then contracts abruptly to localized events or point-like particles when an observation is made.

When unobserved, physical quantum systems behave in wave-like states and only represent tendencies or probabilities of actual events. On the other hand, when an observation is made, the wave-like state changes abruptly, discontinuously, and unpredictably, in a *quantum leap*. At the macro level, the process is seemingly ruled by chance alone, and thus there is the potential for a true choice to be made.

Perception and Reality from a Quantum Viewpoint

All that we see, hear, taste, touch, smell and feel has been created from the data received by our sensory organs. All we ever know of the world around us are the mental constructions we assemble from that data.

However real and external they may seem, these constructions are all phenomena within the mind. This simple fact is very hard to grasp; it goes against all our experience. If there is anything about which we feel certain, it is that the world we experience is real.

We can see, touch and hear it. It seems undeniable that out there, around us, independent and apart from us, exists as a physical world, utterly real, solid and tangible. But the world of our experience is no more *out there* than are our dreams. When we dream, we create a reality in which events happen around us, and in which we perceive other people as individuals separate from us. In the dream it all seems very real. But when we awaken we realize that everything in the dream was actually a creation of our own mind.

The same process of reality-generation occurs in waking consciousness. The difference is that *now* the reality that is created is based on sensory data, and bears a closer relationship to what is taking place in the real world. Nevertheless, however real it may seem, it is not actually, *the real world*. **It is still an image of that world created in the mind.**

The Fabric of Reality – Enter the Age of Conscious Science

The current meta-paradigm of the nature of reality assumes that space, time, and matter constitute the basic framework of reality and consciousness somehow arises from this reality. The truth, it now appears, is the very opposite. As far as the reality we experience is concerned – and this, remember, is the only reality we ever know – consciousness is primary.

Time, space, and matter are secondary; they are aspects of an image of reality manifesting in the mind. They exist within consciousness; not the other way around.

If we consider the reality we experience, then we have to accept that in the final analysis, the new physicists are correct:

Consciousness is the essence of everything – everything in the known universe.

It is the medium from which every aspect of our experience manifests. Every form and quality we ever experience in the world is a construction within consciousness.

What is the Process of Manifestation within the Mind?

How is it that consciousness, which seems so non-material, can take on the material forms that we experience? How do space, time, color, sound, texture, substance, and the many other qualities that we associate with the material world, emerge in consciousness?

Whatever we may be conscious of individually, the *faculty* of consciousness is something we all share. This consciousness is the one truth we cannot deny. It is the absolute certainty of our existence. It is eternal in that it is always there, whatever the contents of our experience. It is the essence of everything we know. And, since every aspect of our experience is a manifestation in the mind, it is the creator of the world we know.

The qualities of truth, absoluteness, eternity, essence, creation are among those traditionally associated with God. From this perspective, the statement, "I am God" is not so puzzling or deluded after all. Although it might be more accurate to say that, "I AM *is* God," or possibly, "God is consciousness."

The text you have just completed needs to be read and re-read as you acquaint yourself with the material. Be patient and remember to enjoy the journey.

Using the Tools of your Mind to Create Reality

Your attention is the source of the creative process in turning your thoughts into reality. Using your intention builds a constant energy toward the reality you want to create. Your body will follow your mind's commands and advance along the way until the desired reality is created.

What is The Law of Attraction?

The law of attraction basically states that you attract in your life circumstances and events that are similar or identical to what you focus your thoughts and beliefs on. Every thought has a vibrational energy pattern that will resonate with similar objects and events that already exist or are coming into existence.

Let's have a practical example to show you how this works. Assume for a moment that you hold the belief that taxes are unnecessary and only create financial problems. What happens is that in your life you will attract circumstances that always feel unpleasant when it comes to the topic of taxes. You may find yourself in a conversation where the topic turns to taxes. Immediately you will feel a shift in how you feel. You may get emotional or you may get upset and in the conversation you may bring up your belief concerning taxes.

As if that isn't enough, when tax season comes you will become more and more nervous with each passing day. Your mind no longer finds rest and ease and even a brief mention of the word *taxes* sucks a huge portion of your attention. In reality, you can experience either positive or negative results.

After filing taxes you may end up receiving a huge return (*positive!*).

Your tax accountant or tax lawyer may call and tell you that there are problems, and you need to bring in additional documents which you don't have *(negative!)*.

How would that scenario play out if you held the belief that taxes are a necessary way to contribute to the betterment of this country? With your tax money more schools can be built and better education can take place within them. You create an attitude where you make enough money to easily pay your taxes each year. You hold a space inside yourself for your tax accountant, and believe that he or she is doing a marvelous job of supporting you getting your taxes done in an easy and effortless manner.

What happens is this, the simple operation of the law of attraction: you will have enough money every year. You will feel good about paying your taxes and they will be done quickly and efficiently. This simply happens because you will attract an outside situation matching your beliefs, attitudes and concepts. Round objects don't fit in square holes! Your energy will always match with similar energy. You will meet people that are on the same wave length that you are. You will attract circumstances in your life that will always match what you think and believe.

A Spiritual Viewpoint of Free Will

I found the following example on one of the exciting audio books from Fred Alan Wolf. Fred Alan Wolf is a physicist and a spiritual seeker, and has dedicated his whole life to the quest of what consciousness truly is.

Imagine that you are sitting on a red elephant. The red elephant symbolizes your higher self, your source, or whatever word you have for it. As you direct your life you tap the elephant on his right ear and the elephant goes right. If you tap him on the left ear he goes left. This is our basic understanding of free will. I decide this and then this happens. It all works fine as long as the elephant goes in the direction you want him to go. However the problem and frustration starts when the elephant turns in another direction – not the one you have chosen.

Here we find ourselves in the realm of hypothesis and speculation:

- Maybe you did something wrong
- Maybe God doesn't want you to take this path
- Maybe you are just not strong enough

The rationalizations we come up with are endless.

What happens on a spiritual level of understanding is the following: The elephant – your higher self – sends you a signal he wants to go right. That could be your intuition, for example. You receive this signal and you align with it and tick the elephant's right ear. Whenever you hear the signal and you follow it, you are absolutely in alignment with your higher self, your source, your infinite power.

Is this still free will you may ask? Yes, it is, as it is still you who is giving yourself the signal.

This is very profound and powerful concept when you truly understand it. All that it takes to operate your life on this level is to explore your consciousness and understand that it is infinite, that it is the ultimate source of your being.

- You are not your mind
- You are not your feelings
- You are not your body
- You are not your thoughts

You are infinite potential; your true essence is beyond space and time. You are everything and nothing at the same time. You were never born and you will never die. You are the spirit that is shared with every other living form on this planet. You have access to anything and everything you wish to have.

The Ultimate Question
Free Will Versus Destiny?

There is a question that is centuries old, still as baffling today as it was when it was first asked. Do we have free will or is everything predetermined?

Many people find their answers somewhere in between these two extremes. They believe that we have free will and also that there is something bigger than who we are, something that operates somehow on a more fundamental level of reality that has the ability to predetermine how we live our lives to a greater or lesser extent. However that still leaves you questioning where you have control and where you do not. The effect of this dilemma is that most people really don't know what they can and cannot create and change in their lives.

It leads ultimately to crazy outcomes like war that are fought in the name of God.

When it comes to the issue of control in and of itself, understand that there are three different universes:

- The universe of yourself
- The universe of others
- The universe of the material world

All three have their own rules and the biggest obstacle to success in your life is understanding the rules of each universe. Failure in life always has to with these three universes and the mix up of each of them.

For example, you might want to be more patient with yourself. Of course, the way to handle this is ultimately in your own universe. So you might, for example, start a meditation class or you might contemplate bigger things like the age and the size of the universe. That would shift the perspective of your current level of patience. However, the wrong way would be to put the focus on others, telling them to do things faster or criticizing them for something, which shifts the focus off of you, where it really needs to be.

Another example: Let's say you want people in your neighborhood to be more conscious with their trash and to start recycling their cans and bottles. Here is what you would do when you handle it within your own universe. Every time you see some of your neighbors piling recycling in their normal trash, you tell them how wrong it is and that they should recycle it the way you do. You might even talk with your friends and complain about how unconsciousness these people are and how frustrated you are with them. You see that everything that you do is just a projection of your own universe.

If you want to handle it properly, you'll need to get into *their* universe. For example, you could announce a gathering in your neighborhood and provide a powerful presentation about recycling. You could show them where their trash lands; you could show them the impact lots of trash has in nature and you could also show them what happens when trash is recycled. For example, you could include information about the growing recycling industry in Europe and how it supports the entire region by making the technology and techniques available everywhere.

And last but not least, what happens exactly when you want something to occur in the physical universe and you handle it in the universe of others? Let's assume that you build a house and that you hire a contractor to do it. Soon, you find that things are going horribly wrong. You blame the contractor, but the contractor just ignores you and tells you to shut up or face additional delays or cost overruns. You have no choice but to live with the situation.

When you handle this situation in the right universe you are the one who is ultimately in charge here, not the contractor. The contractor is an outcome of your concepts and beliefs. Instead of blaming him you could go back into your universe and handle the situation from there. You could ask yourself what you may have done to create this situation. You understand that you are 100% responsible for what is happening. You may not have set the right goals, or been too vague about the details. You may have had your priorities and attention somewhere else. Whatever the reasons, there is a possible overall solution that will resolve the situation.

It all comes down to fully recognizing that you are the creator and that no one else can be blamed for your creation. Blaming others is denying taking responsibility as the creator of this situation. It is telling yourself a lie over and over again if you never take such responsibility.

Everything starts in your own universe with your own thoughts. When you get lost take a break and find your way back home to yourself. Reconnect with your true source of power.

Conclusion:
You have free will; however it all comes down to either accepting who you are or denying it. This is the one choice you can truly make from the source of your consciousness. Either you accept the path that you have chosen already or you resist it.

If you accept this path, all the choices you make come from the source of your consciousness and you will know with certainty that it is your higher self telling you what to do. You can say that on that level, you are not making any choices at all, you are just aligning with your path.

If you don't accept your past, your choices are made from the ego and do not align with your higher self. Therefore, the choices you make will neither support your self nor will they be good choices for anyone else.

This is the path of isolation that leads many people into depression. It is a path that is cut off from the unlimited life force. Spirit has no opportunity here to nourish and be nourished and to manifest good.

Intention – Aim For Your Goals

Intention refers to what one plans to do or achieve. Intention simply signifies a course of action that one proposes to follow: It is my intention to take a vacation next month. So you could say your attention is charged with a mindset that directs itself towards accomplishing something.

A wonderful book I highly recommend is *The Power Of Intention* by Wayne Dyer. Dr. Dyer outlines seven essential rules in his book that provide the groundwork for powerful intentions. This book is also available as an audio book as well as in DVD form.

Let's assume that one day you wake up in the morning and you don't have any intentions. What would happen? Absolutely nothing – you probably would stay in bed until you needed to eat something or you may have to go to the bathroom. That means that some outer circumstances, perhaps the biologic processes – which are, after all, *bodily intentions* – generate your moving. Without *intention* you would never accomplish anything, not even the simplest task.

You may not be aware of your intentions as you find yourself getting up and out of bed automatically, as you 'want' or 'need' to go to work. So some of your intentions are operating without you being aware of them.

However, in this context we are talking about *deliberate intentions*. You get up and out of bed and you think and contemplate what you would like to accomplish today. You think about your goals in life and intend to make them happen. Following through on your intentions is a very active process that gives your life a direction. By setting and realigning your intentions you will achieve your goals and fulfill your dreams.

Is Setting a Goal the Same as Having an Intention?

They are similar, but not the same. You can set as many goals as you want, however, if you don't have an intention to achieve any of them – they will never happen. An intention is much more powerful than simply setting a goal in life. Intentions will allow you to reach any goal. A goal is a subject; it is something that is happening in the future. An intention includes this and adds a driving force to it. This driving force is always in the present and will determine the outcome of your action.

How to Make Powerful Intentions

We use intention to guide our attention in a new direction in order to create a new or different reality. For example, maybe you'd like to change your job. Most people start with the intent of having a better job, as the old one is not satisfying anymore. However, trouble may be brewing here already . . .

If you move on from something you don't like to something you prefer, you may deny your current situation. In order to make successful intentions, it is important to deal with the current situation first, while doing some analytical thinking about it.

Again, the key is to take full responsibility, and to understand that you are the only person responsible for the current circumstances.

Do away with any judgments of your current situation, until you can see it from a neutral perspective. There was a point in your life when it was the perfect decision. Don't compare the present moment with your past, as you have since had new experiences and gained a more complete perspective that additional experience in this area brings.

This is a common mistake in thinking; it is like a loophole in the mind. You jump from one timeline to another timeline, and then compare the two. This leads to false conclusions. Leave the past behind – don't reinvent it!

Creativity is never a response from the past; it is always a creative act in the now.

Evaluate your Current Situation

If you look at your current situation without judgment, you are able to see and analyze your life. Only from a neutral standpoint can you make a powerful new decision. This new decision will be based on deliberate intent instead of reacting to circumstance. This is where choice and free will come in.

There is a very interesting scene in one of the old Star Trek movies. The spaceship *Enterprise* somehow got too close to a black hole and its powerful engines were incapable of escaping the crushing gravity of the black hole.

The whole crew, including Commander James Kirk, were fearfully awaiting their impending deaths. Everyone was focused on what would certainly happen in short order when the *Enterprise* was sucked into the black hole. Alone of all the crew, Spock stood patiently observing the current situation on the big monitor screen.

Spock voiced his thoughts on the dire situation in one succinct statement: "Fascinating." McCoy, the ship's doctor, exploded in nervous anger, "What in the hell is *fascinating* about the fact that we are all dying in a few moments?" Spock, calmly replies, "*The way it will happen.*"

This perfectly illustrates my point here. We have one person who is observing the current situation without judgment and therefore still has free attention to make choices. All the others are consumed by fear – they are without choice – or *choice-less* – in the matter.

Of course, the story has a happy ending as Spock finds a way to save the *Enterprise* and the ship's complement of 400 crew. Spock was the only one capable of this valiant act as he was able to analyze the current situation from a neutral point of view.

From the perspective of being neutral, you can ask yourself the following questions:

- What do I like about my current job?
- What do I want to improve in my next job?
- What would be the perfect job for me?
- What would I like to feel from my next job?
- What am I good at?
- In which areas is this job supporting me to live my full potential?

Write down the answers to these questions, and start to write out a few full sentences based on your answers. Include all the positive points. Make these sentences as precise as possible.

An example statement might read something like this: "My next job is exciting; it flows with me, makes me happy, and I am able to learn and grow from it.

When you are done, read it out loud. If you have trouble saying the sentence, or even memorizing it, then it is not ready. Simply take a few moments and refine it.

Overcoming Pitfalls when Creating Intentions

Intentions are formed in your conscious mind; however, it's your subconscious that receives these commands and creates the necessary opportunities in your life. In other words, your conscious mind decides on this new opportunity – creating a new reality.

- Use only positive words
- Include a time frame
- Remove negations
- Be precise

Here is a simple test. Don't think about a blue elephant! What happened? You thought about the blue elephant, you may have even imagined it. The subconscious does not work analytically. It cannot understand words like 'don't' or 'not.' It works mostly in images, sounds, and smells.

You want to avoid the use of any negative words in your intentions. Always formulate your intentions in such a way that they reflect the outcome of what you'd like to create.

Example of how not to do it:
- I don't want to have so much responsibility.

Better example:
- In my new job I feel comfortable with my responsibilities.

Include a Time Frame:

There is a difference between creating in your own universe and creating in the physical world. When you create inside yourself there is no time involved – your consciousness is timeless!

For example, if you'd like to change your attitude toward your boss, you don't need to set a time frame. You can simply create the intention: "I appreciate my boss," or, "I value my boss's viewpoints and beliefs." It will work instantly if there is no other belief or intention in its way.

When you deal with the physical world, setting a time frame becomes important. The physical world works within time and space. If you build a new house, first you have a plan, and then you move dirt, assemble wood, install plumbing and move furniture until the house is complete. It takes time and effort.

So if you make your intention but you leave out the time frame – your intention becomes doubtful. For example: "I am working in my dream job." Well, you would probably say right away: "I'm not!" It sounds more like an affirmation than an intention. Include the time frame, and this example turns into: "I am working in my dream job, six months from now."

Pay attention to any reactions you have when you formulate your intention. Your mind may interfere and tell you: "No way, I will never get this," or "this is impossible." If you encounter these instant judgments, formulate your intentions differently, so that they feel more do-able. Sometimes you may want to break a big intention into smaller pieces.

For example: "In two weeks I am a millionaire," is an intention that may not work for most people. However, an intention like: "Every day I have more money to spend," may get you there sooner than you think.

New Year's Intentions Versus Birthday Intentions

Many people make New Year's resolutions, which is a good thing. However, making them on your birthday is more efficient.

Why is this? A new year is an artificial point of time, it just means that one year passed, and is not related to you in any way – it's impersonal. If you make your new year's resolution on your birthday, it is personal, because on this specific day the sun is in the same position as it was when you were born. Astrologers call this point a sun-sun conjunction. It is a very powerful point in time, as a new individual cycle starts for you.

Creating Your Intentions – Worksheet

Personal Development:

Health:

Relationships:

Career:

Financial & Wealth:

Sport & Hobbies:

Community & Charity:

Why Your Attitude Makes A Difference

A reporter was sent to a stone cutter to interview three different men doing exactly the same job – hammering stones. Asking about how they liked their job, the first one answers, "I really hate it. I barely make the money to survive. I am doing the same stupid thing over and over. My back hurts, I am getting old, and I absolutely see no sense in what I am doing."

The second man responds to the same question, saying, "It's not bad, I have a decent house and a nice car. I love my family; however, I am not fulfilled with what I am doing."

The third man replies, "I love my job. I am absolutely thrilled and I appreciate everyday I can be here. I think my work is wonderful as all these stones I am hammering will later be part of the material to build a wonderful cathedral. A place where many people can worship God and a place where many people will find the strength to overcome struggles and difficulties in their lives. I cannot imagine doing something different – I feel happy every moment."

Remember – all these people are doing the same exact work. It is only their attitude that makes a completely different person out of them. Not only are these people all different, they each will be affecting the other people around them by their attitudes.

It's the basic principle of looking at a half full or half empty glass. It is your viewpoint of life that determines you attitude. If you think everything has to be given to you for free, you are setting yourself up for big disappointment. You will spend a lot of time being angry because you'll soon discover that nothing comes to you for free. Focusing on who you are and what you have will shift your attitude and make you more humble. Recognize what you do have in life. Go out in nature and recognize the beauty of life. Pick a flower, watch and feel the grace of it.

Conclusion – The Art of Manifesting

Let's bring everything together you have learned so far. Know that fulfilling your dreams is the purpose of your life. It is exercising your strengths and talents to contribute to the greater good of all. Know that fulfilling your dreams is your destiny. Never ever give anybody permission to take this powerful force away from you.

- ***Decide what you want in life. This may change during your life, so evaluate your goals and dreams every few years. Align with your long-term goals and adjust your short-term goals.***

- ***Know your strengths, talents and gifts. Also know your weak areas, exercise your strengths and get help from others for your weak areas. Have you thought about a mentor?***

- ***Understand that you have unlimited attention. Decide where you want to put your attention. Limit the areas where you waste your attention. Increase the areas where you want results.***

- ***Use your imagination as a virtual playing field. Imagine what it feels like to have reached your goals. Imagine what it feels like when you live your dreams.***

- ***Contemplate your beliefs. Your beliefs create reality. Replace non-supporting beliefs with beliefs that support your goals and dreams.***

- *Craft powerful intentions that state your life dreams.*

- *Understand that what you hold in your consciousness attracts similar circumstances in your life.*

Use a Vision Board to Manifest Your Dreams

Buy a large cork board and start pinning up your dreams. Use words and pictures that show exactly what you want in life. Put this board in a place where you can see it every day. Spend some time every day and let any imaginative thoughts and feelings flow through you.

How to Set Your Goals And Dreams on Autopilot

Don't you feel it is time for you to step forward and take full control of your potential? There is now a remarkably simple solution for manifesting your goals, dreams and desires in life. A software program that supports and guides you in manifesting exactly what you want.

If you work on the computer you can use the Dream Manifestation Wizard™, software specially developed to help you manifest your dreams. It is like having an electronic dream board and it is much more flexible then a simple board on the wall.

The Dream Manifestation Wizard™ creates an exact blueprint in your subconscious of what you want to manifest. Your subconscious mind will immediately start to work on turning your dream into reality, applying the latest discoveries in quantum physics shifting and directing your attention toward new possibilities. Acting on these possibilities will finally bring your dreams to life.

What the Dream Manifestation Kit™ Will Do For You

The Dream Manifestation Wizard™ will help you shape your life exactly the way you want it.

- Learn to set habits for creating abundance and prosperity
- Develop a laser sharp focus to target your goals & desires
- Achieve financial freedom and live an extraordinary life
- Pinpoint your talents and passions
- Rewire your brain to make success inevitable
- Make the right decisions with confidence and certainty
- Learn a new revitalizing, life changing way of thinking
- Develop a positive attitude towards your life and others
- Imprint your personal success formula on your consciousness
- Develop extraordinary imagination power
- Find your life partner and create authentic relationships
- Learn how to contribute to a green and sustainable world
- Rely on yourself instead on economy and government
- Make powerful life decisions using your intuition

The Ultimate Life Fulfillment
Serving Others

If you cultivate your strengths and talents you will find new ways to use them in your life. Your work situation will reflect and include them more frequently. Ultimately you are serving others, and serving others is the ultimate purpose and the greatest achievement in life.

By serving others you will feel abundance and prosperity in your life without any effort. It will come to you as a result of doing the right thing.

Serving others will shift your focus beyond yourself. It will give your life meaning and a sense that there are worthwhile things greater than yourself. It will free you from thinking about yourself and by serving others you will find true lasting happiness. You will understand that serving others is your life purpose and you are doing it because you cannot do otherwise. It is a natural process. It is the ultimate purpose of consciousness itself.

Consciousness strives to evolve, to constantly improve things. Ultimately, this evolved consciousness will achieve the greater goal of being part of an enlightened planetary civilization where we all live in harmony with each other.

It does not matter how far you as an individual, or our current civilization as a whole are away from this goal. Time does not hold any meaning for consciousness. Just think about how far we have come, thus far.

If we were to imagine the age of this earth as a day, humans will have just appeared in the world within the few seconds, and we have just started to explore consciousness within the last second.

May all your dreams come true . . .

Helpful Resources For Your Personal Development

The following books and movies are a great source of inspiration and will further help you on your way to manifesting your dreams. Choose what inspires you in the moment. Come back to this list every month and you may find another book that will then be ready to be explored.

Most importantly: use the knowledge of these books and experience the benefits. If you don't try new things you will never find out what's in it for you. Understanding it is one thing – living it is another!